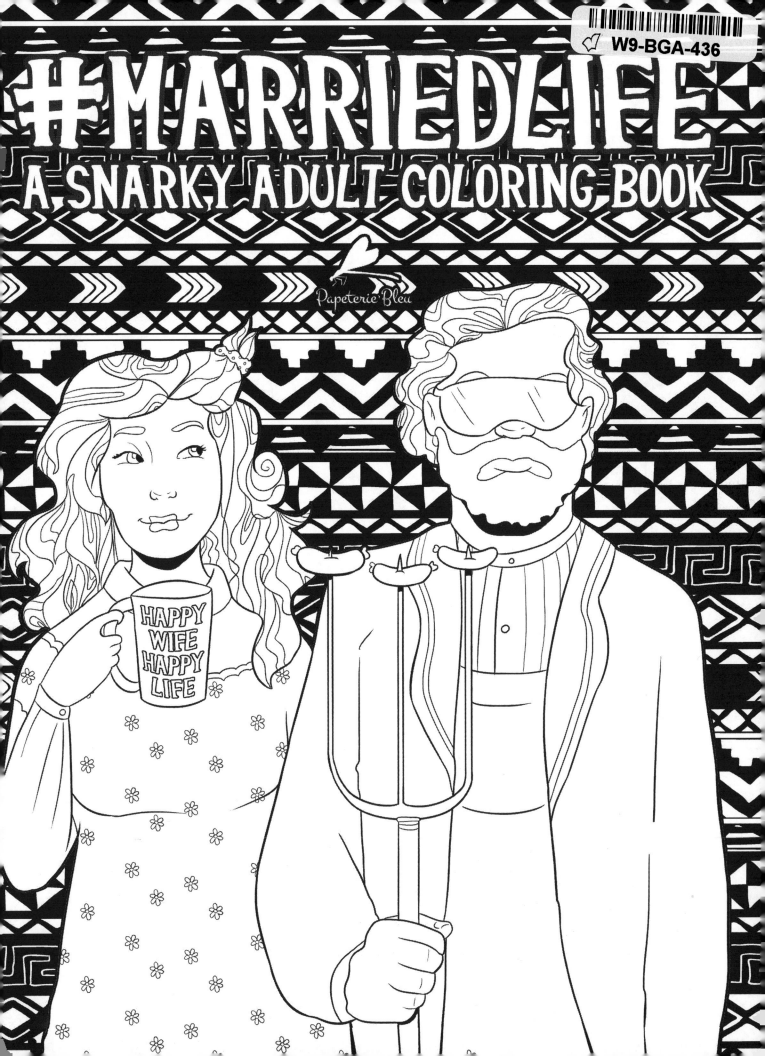

Illustrated by Micaela

ISBN-13: 978-1945888908
ISBN-10: 1945888903

MY HUSBAND ASKED ME TO WHISPER DIRTY THINGS IN HIS EAR, SO I WHISPERED: *kitchen, bathroom, living room*

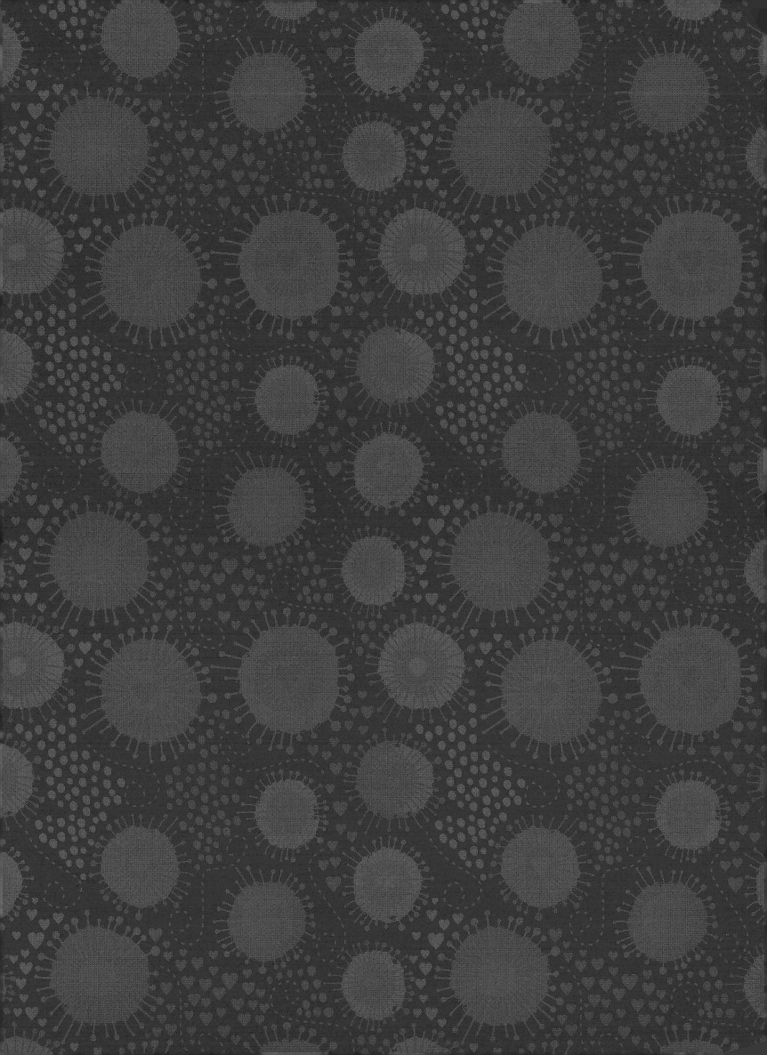

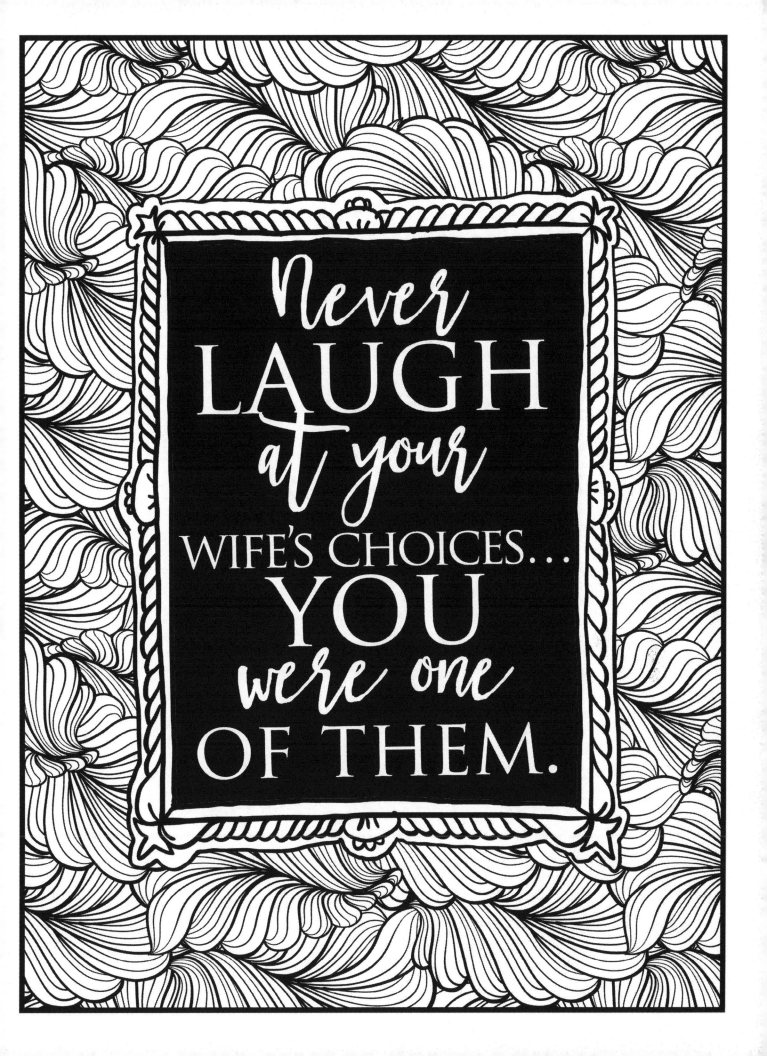

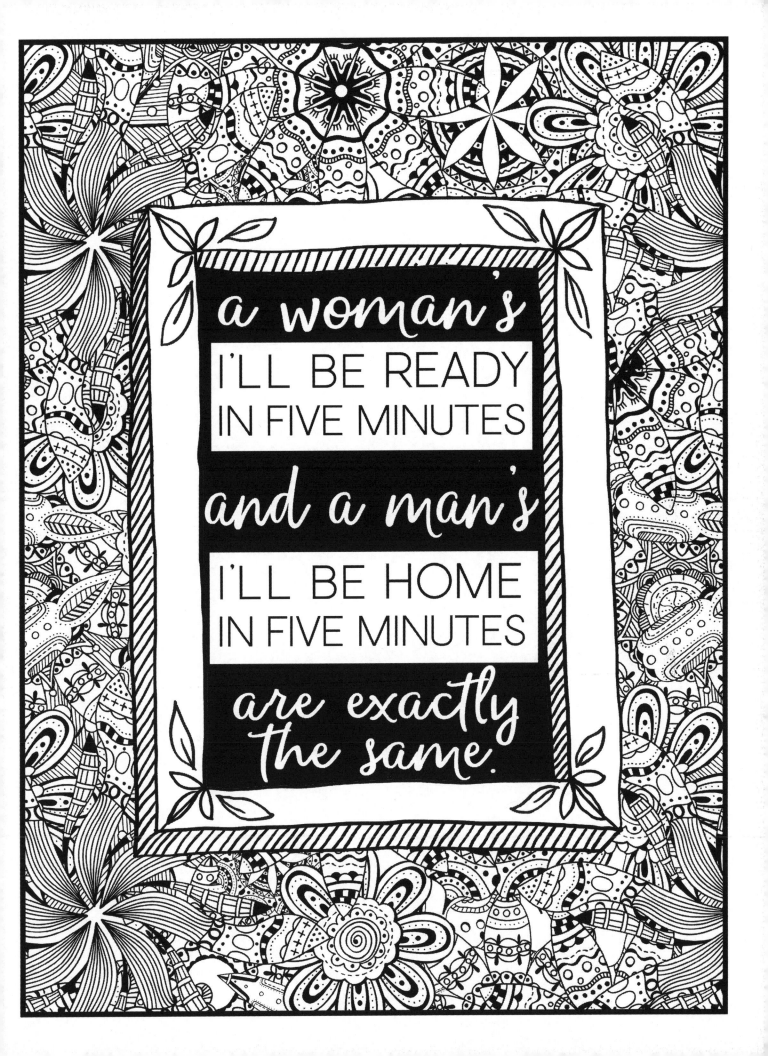

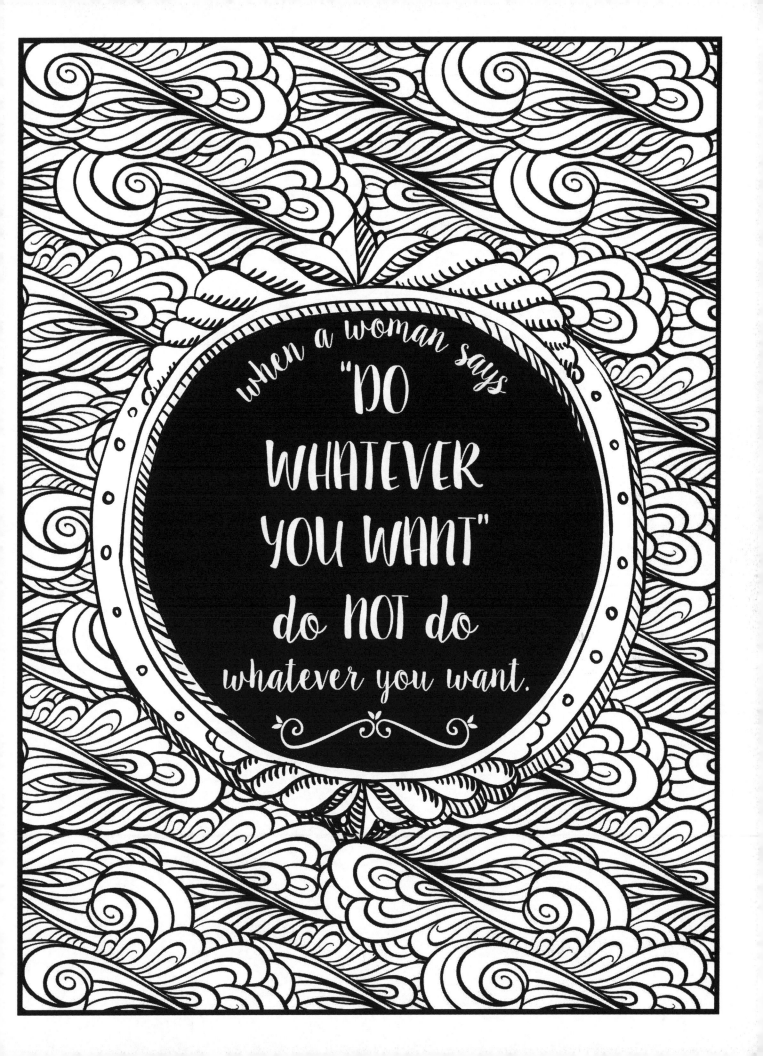

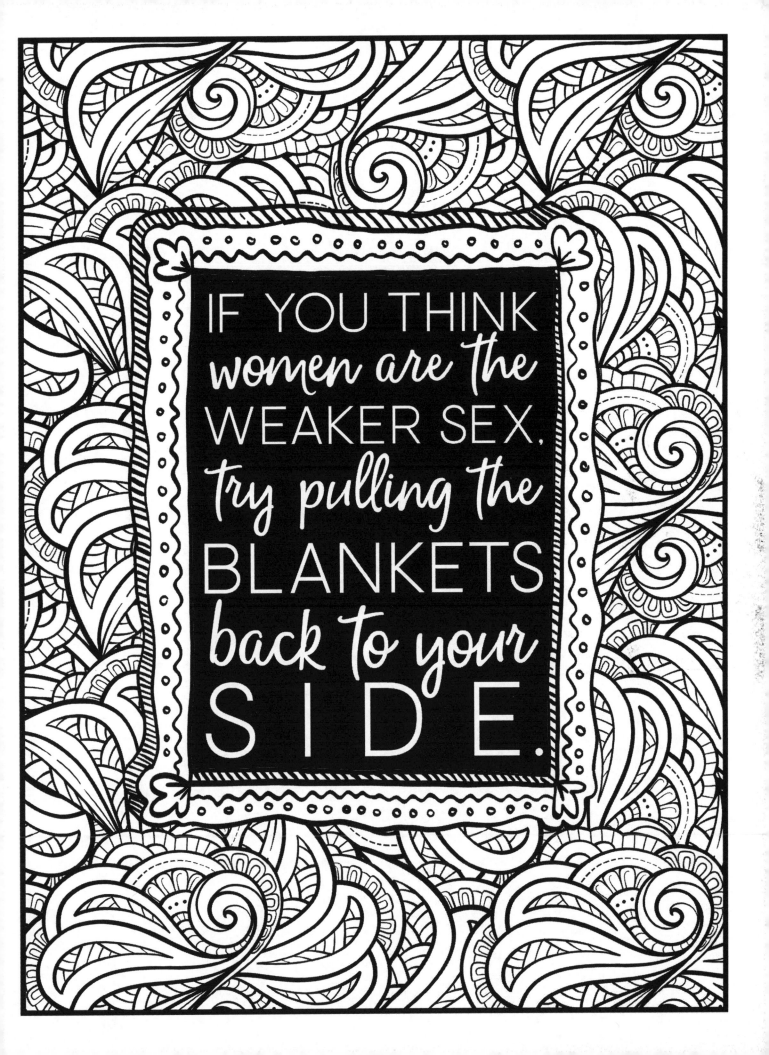

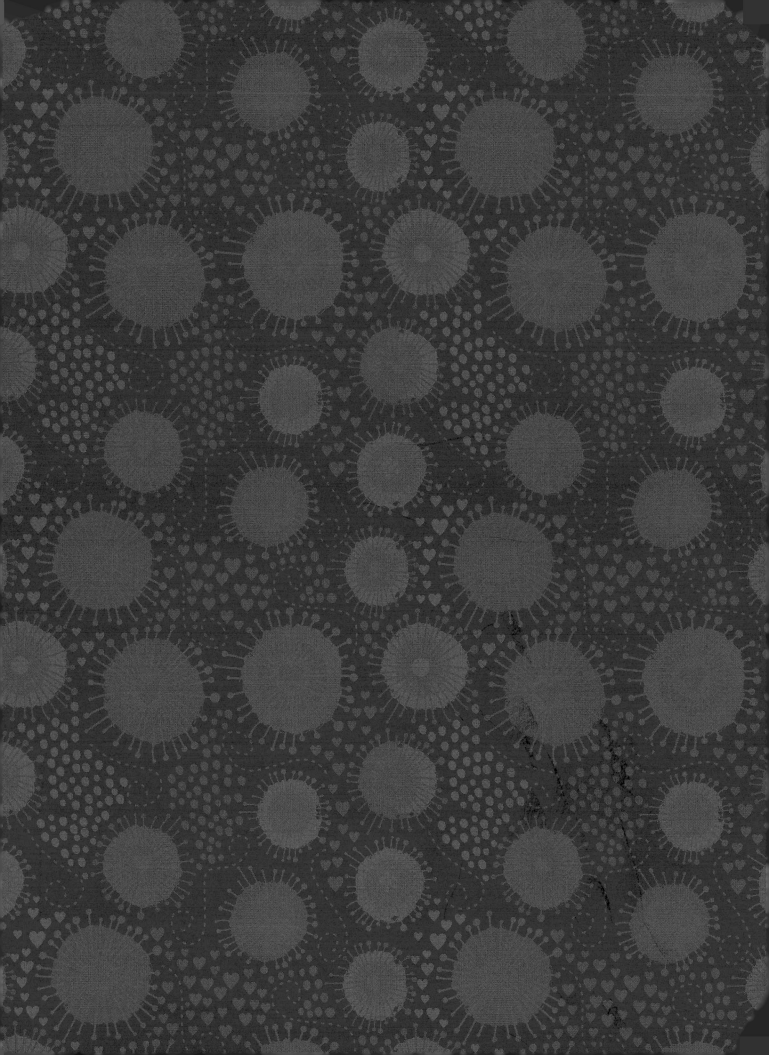

★ MARRIAGE ADVICE ★
IF YOU must fight FIGHT NAKED!

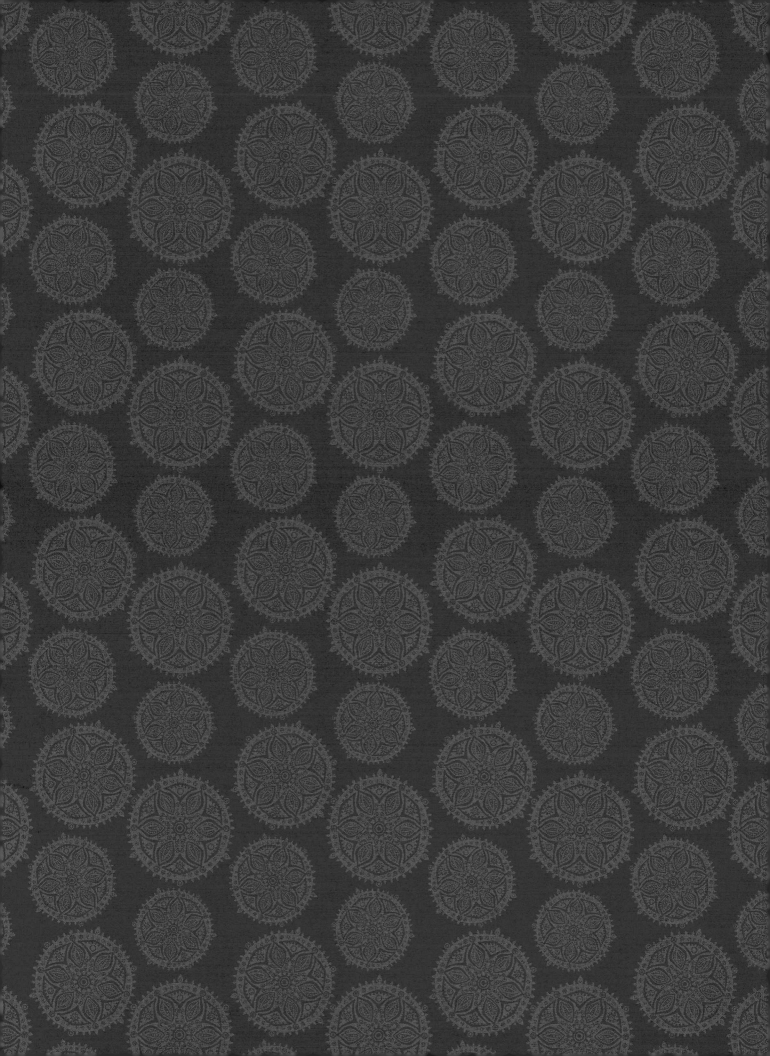

BE SURE TO FOLLOW US
ON SOCIAL MEDIA FOR THE
LATEST NEWS, SNEAK
PEEKS, & GIVEAWAYS

📷 @PapeterieBleu

f Papeterie Bleu

🐦 @PapeterieBleu

ADD YOURSELF TO OUR MONTHLY
NEWSLETTER FOR FREE DIGITAL
DOWNLOADS AND DISCOUNT CODES

www.papeteriebleu.com/newsletter

CHECK OUT OUR OTHER BOOKS!

www.papeteriebleu.com

   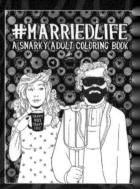

CHECK OUT OUR OTHER BOOKS!

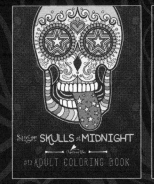

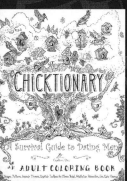

CHECK OUT OUR OTHER BOOKS!

www.papeteriebleu.com

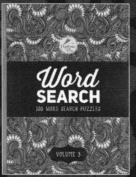
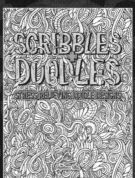

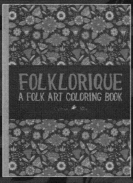
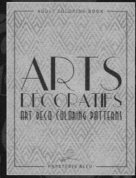